Final Act of Ownership

Selling Your Small Business

First Edition

Jerry Baltus

Final Act of Ownership
Selling Your Small Business

This book may be ordered through booksellers or by contacting:

Jerry Baltus
2309 Fairfield Lane
Plymouth, WI 53073
920-449-5130
jkbaltusgroup@wi.rr.com

Published by:
Fritz & Amber Publishing
Plymouth, WI

Final Act of Ownership
Selling Your Small Business
By Jerry Baltus

Contents

Preface

The very first client I worked with on developing an exit strategy for his business was very guarded about engaging a business coach. He had a successful business that had served his life over his entire working career. A couple of years prior to our work together, he was approached by an out-of-state business broker who had offered to do a valuation of his business for $10,000. The valuation was done and they signed a broker agreement to work on finding a buyer at or close to the valued amount. That was the last my client heard of the broker in spite of numerous phone and email attempts to contact them. The broker obviously had no intention of actually working to help sell the business, but rather sought only the transaction fee for the valuation. Not only was my client ripped off by this unscrupulous "broker", he was also made suspicious of all future offerings of professional help to achieve his goal of a successful business sale. Thus began my interest in providing real help to small business owners who feel ready to cash in on the equity value they've built.

In serving small and midsize businesses as a business coach, I encounter a wide variety of skill sets, business acumen, goals and outlook among these business owners. Some seem to coast through to great success with their business, while most struggle to keep the business viable. Somewhat surprisingly, most owners don't want to be entrepreneurial superstars. They simply want the business to provide the kind of income that permits a reasonable lifestyle to enjoy the things that are truly more important than their business, i.e. family, friends, recreation, and spiritual pursuits among others. They also desire that the business builds the kind of wealth and equity that will be meaningful in their retirement years.

The reality is that most businesses struggle to support the owners' lives to the degree they desire. We've often heard the statistics about high failure rates of small businesses in their early years. But in addition we see evidence that for businesses that survive, the majority are not viewed by their owners as being in the category of "thriving". Yet we're a proud lot, we American business owners. We value our independence and self-sufficiency, and seldom reach out to others for advice, support or help. As a business coach, I often sense that there exists a "stigma" against seeking help. Yet, when that help is given there is often a sense of relief and a new beginning.

This book is not about the variety of ways business coaching can support the vast market of small businesses. There is plenty of literature and helpful resources available on that, and more and more business owners are coming to the realization that a business coach is a wise investment in their future success. Statistics show that working with a coach early on usually produces a higher value business in the long term. Slowly, the culture is becoming more accepting of the kind of synergy that a business coach can create working with small business owners.

One element that seems lacking to this market of small business owners is resources related to selling the business. This book is about providing some perspective, some thoughtful subject matter, and some guidance to help navigate this final act of business ownership. Most other aspects of owning a business can be learned by trial and error, although I don't recommend that method. If the errors aren't too serious, the business may survive, the owner will be wiser for the experience, and a different approach will be used the next time, likely producing a better result. However, selling your business is something you typically only get one shot at. It is the one aspect of ownership that helps you achieve that wealth and equity goal that we universally desire as we approach retirement.

Of course, there are good advisors who can help with the process, but often they are excellent at only a small portion of the effort, and may not help maximize your overall sales potential. We've found that for businesses with valuation under $1.5 million, fewer resources such as brokers and investment bankers are available to market these entities to motivated buyers. So to some extent, small business owners are again left to their own devices to figure out how to position, value, market and sell the asset that they've spent most of their career building.

To make matters worse, there is a decline in the numbers of businesses that are transferred to the next generation of the owner's family. For one thing, families are typically smaller today, and the kids may not wish to follow in Mom or Dad's footsteps, particularly if they've seen them struggle and stress over the financial and lifestyle "merits" of business ownership.

But all is not lost! There are many reasons to be optimistic about crossing the finish line of business ownership by completing a successful sale of your ongoing concern to a new, motivated owner. For one thing, entrepreneurship is alive and well in our country and many people and existing businesses are seeking valuable entities to "take to the next level".

According to the US Census Bureau, there were 7.4 million business establishments in the United States in 2011. Of these, 7.2 million, or 97.7%, employed less than 100 employees, leaving only 167,000 (2.3%) businesses employing 100 employees or greater. Even more compelling, 5.4 million, or **73.6% employed less than 10 employees**. But wait.... these statistics don't include solopreneurs, those who work for themselves without any employees. The Census Bureau calls these businesses "nonemployers" and they total **22.5 million** entities! So, if we look at all business entities in our country with **less than 10 employees**, we have a pool consisting of **27.9 million small (what some might call 'micro') businesses**.

Business ownership remains an attractive goal and it is achieved not only via startups, but by the transfer of existing businesses. For those small business owners banking on the sale of their business or the equity value built into it to fund their retirement, there is reason for optimism about the attractiveness of the firm and the ability to find a budding entrepreneur to take it over.

Selling your small business is not dramatically different than selling a large business, sometimes even a bit simpler. Yes, resources to help with the process will be more limited, but there are many good professionals who can be trusted. It is my hope that this book can provide some guidance and knowledge that will make the process more understandable.

The one piece of advice that cannot be overstated is the recommendation to start early! Please don't wait until the last minute, or even the last month or year prior to retirement to start the sales process, as you stand a high chance of being disappointed. Your business, no matter how small, is likely worth something, so don't lock the doors and walk away. Reach out to others (like a business coach with exit strategy experience) and lay out a plan that suits you and your business, to give it the chance to continue under the legacy you've started.

Chapter 1 - Emotions of the Owner/Seller

You've been thinking about selling your business for a long time, haven't you? Chances are, you've forgotten when you first had that thought. For most business owners, the initial thought about selling occurs when they start their business! Think back to when you began. Didn't you have the thought of "I'll make this business worth $X and retire comfortably"? Or, "My kids can join me in this business one day and buy me out when I'm ready to step aside"? Or how about, "I'll hire some great people and give them first chance to buy the business so that they can enjoy the security and financial rewards we will build together"?

Almost all of us have those thoughts at the beginning stages of business, but often forget about them as we get immersed in the day-to-day running of the enterprise. Then as we approach retirement, those selling thoughts re-emerge as we try to evaluate our options and future. But there is a difference in the emotions that come with these thoughts at the start of business versus the latter stages. At business start-up, thoughts of selling the business elicit emotions of hope, desire, optimism and even confidence.

But close to a selling event, the emotions usually experienced are fear, uncertainty, anxiety, and regret.

Sounds backwards, doesn't it? Well, backwards or not, emotions often get in the way of rational and wise actions. Negative emotions, especially, have the effect of stopping our actions altogether, leaving us paralyzed against taking the steps we once dreamed of. One of the first things to examine and understand when approaching the sale of your business, is what is going on with these emotions.

FEAR

President Franklin Roosevelt's profound quote, "...the only thing we have to fear is fear itself" summarizes the problem with this powerful emotion of fear. The corollary is that by pushing through fear, by examining the source of fear and by looking at options, we can often find that there is really very little to fear in the first place. And so it is with selling your business.

For most, selling a business is a one-time event. Unless you are a serial entrepreneur, you haven't experienced this before. You know how to do everything your business requires to be successful in its day-to-day running, but you don't know where to start when it comes to selling it. You have few options and only one shot at turning your business asset into your retirement asset, and you don't know how to go about it. That is fear producing!

At the same time, most business owners don't really know what their business is worth. That uncertainty raises the prospect of either overselling or underselling the business, which causes the fears of embarrassment or criticism.

Similarly, many business owners face the prospect of its value being very low, or even zero. Imagine spending a large part of your life invested both financially and emotionally in your enterprise, and fearing that there is no financial reward for your efforts. For those who dreamed that their business would be their retirement fund, the inability to harvest a meaningful value from it can produce the fear of poverty.

Another common concern resides in owners who have created a business that revolves completely around them, and it is the fear that no one else can run the enterprise. Not knowing what to do about that.... not trusting others to manage certain aspects of the operation.... not knowing how to delegate, train or hire appropriately are all causes of this fear that the business can't survive without them.

In spite of all this not knowing, business owners are also reluctant to reach out to experts and advisers for help. Part of this is anxiety about whom to trust. Part of it is a learned trait of "going it alone" that many in business have adapted in order to keep expenses low. Unfortunately, unscrupulous advisers who cause businesses to invest in their often unfulfilled services, create distrust of all advisers, thus causing more uncertainty and rejection of even the good sources of help and advice.

The antidote to fear is rooted in action. The table below provides advice as to the antidote for types of fear that often come with selling a business. It's important to take some first steps, baby steps in most cases, to allow yourself a chance to learn that the fears experienced are mostly unfounded. In talking to others, getting some education, examining options and planning, the fear emotions start to be replaced with knowledge, teamwork and confidence.

FEAR	ANTIDOTE
Have never sold a business before	Get education and advice from experienced pros
Not knowing what the business is worth	Obtain a valuation and discuss with an adviser
The business has no value	Start early to change the operation to build value
No one but the owner can run the business	Learn to delegate, educate, hire and trust others
The "experts" cannot be trusted	Build a network to help find trusted advisers

ENERGY LEVEL

William had always worked hard. This one trait of his got him through the hard times in his business. It was a source of pride and even a competitive advantage. He felt he could always run circles around his competitors, even if they seemed stronger in other aspects of the business. William loved working hard and through most of his career felt that he would be able to work this way indefinitely. But in the last year or two, something changed. His friends talked more about retirement plans. William had managed to take his wife, Judy, on a few more vacations in recent years and they talked of how nice it was to be able to get away from the business and enjoy these simple trips. Whether because of these things, or in addition to them, William felt his energy level declining. His interest in working as hard as he did in his earlier years was not so strong anymore. He felt distracted, disengaged, unmotivated. One day he called a business broker he'd heard about and decided to put the business up for sale.

You might not think Energy Level belongs in a chapter about Emotions. However, emotions are really nothing more than thoughts. It is our thinking that ultimately affects our motivation, or energy level. So these two issues are actually quite closely related, and we can theoretically control both by our thoughts. But most business owners, having the control and discipline to maintain a high energy level throughout their career, often lose it by giving up prematurely.

There is nothing wrong with William's decision to sell his business, nor his timing. But now William has one of two paths he can take. He can either push the broker to try to get a fast sale resulting in a presumably low price or he can muster an even higher energy level to prepare the business for sale at its full value. The energy level, consistency and discipline that made the business successful in the first place are even more critical at the end of ownership if the owner is going to realize a liquidation value respecting the business equity. The effort is worth it because the added value in terms of the sale price is almost always substantial. Isn't it worth it to make that one, final push of effort to make sure you capitalize fully on your business nest egg?

LEGACY & CULTURE

Studies and stories about the small business sales process often touch on the emergence of the seller's strong desire that the new buyer continue the traditions and culture of the business. This emotional desire stems partly from a pride of wanting what has been built to continue, thus feeding the legacy of the selling owner. It is often a factor in the desire to bring offspring into the business to carry on what the parent has built. It is also based on the emotional ties with employees, customers and suppliers.

But there is also a compelling business reason to desire a continuance of the seller's culture. Culture (the values, beliefs and guiding principles of the organization) has a strong bearing on the kind of employees the business has, as well as being a key reason that customers are loyal to the firm. So changing the culture not only undermines the seller's legacy, but also risks the very business itself.

A common emotion among sellers is the desire to take care of its employees and customers. After all, they've spent years accepting responsibility for the well-being of employees and those employees have been a major factor in their success. The seller probably has developed close relationships with customers who depend on the business for their own success. That sense of responsibility carries over into the business sale process and can affect who the seller accepts as the future owner of their business.

It is important for a seller to realize that sometimes culture can and should be maintained and sometimes it may be beneficial to "let it go". For example, if the business will be absorbed as a division or product line of a bigger company, it will be nearly impossible for that sense of culture to be maintained. Yet this type of "strategic buyer" (see Chapter 2) may be exactly the opportunity to maximize the value for the seller. In that case, insisting on holding out for a better culturally-aligned buyer could result in a lower valuation, or even the inability to sell at all. Thus the emotions of this difficult culture vs. value tradeoff need to be discussed and assessed.

A sense of legacy is also linked to culture when it comes to the emotions of a business sale. The seller has worked hard to create a valuable business that not only supports their life, but also contributes to the economy, supports employees and customers, provides a unique product or service experience and brings them personal recognition and stature. Selling the business brings with it the fear of being forgotten as the one who toiled to bring the business to a successful state.

Dealing with the culture and legacy emotions of a business sale is best done by starting early to define and position the business to carry these forward without the current owner. Discussing culture with employees and sharing stories about the history of the business are good ways to start. Planning sessions that include definitions of Purpose or Values are helpful, along with the strategic path that the organization sees as its direction. Likewise, marketing materials that recognize the achievements and past results not only help to attract customers who value the company's efforts, but also become part of the legacy of the firm.

Sharing the emotions related to selling your business is useful to the professionals who guide you, and even to a prospective buyer. It is especially helpful to you, the seller, because it makes the emotions a healthy part of the process, instead of a barrier to doing things that are in your best interest.

Chapter 2 - Buyers

It's useful to think about types of buyers as your business is being prepared for sale. After all, just as you would consider target customers for your business as you develop effective marketing plans, targeting buyers helps to give direction to your message and your valuation in the sales process.

The structure, size, and profitability of the business, among other factors, help to determine the kind of buyer that might be attracted to the business and able to carry on its success, and even improve it. At the risk of oversimplifying, think of buyers as being defined in three categories:

- Individual buyers
- Financial buyers
- Strategic buyers

INDIVIDUAL BUYERS

Typical of our image of the American entrepreneur, individual buyers embody the risk-taking, confident, visionary talent of successful business owners. For many sellers, the type of buyer most often imagined is someone exactly like the individual seller. After all, who better to carry on what has been built than to find someone with the same background, technical knowledge and culture of the seller? However, taking the business forward may actually require different skills, and a different outlook than those skills that brought the business this far. Finding someone just like the seller who also possesses the entrepreneurial desire and financial ability to purchase, can often prove to be quite difficult.

Let's look at three different types of individual buyers: Technicians, Managers and Entrepreneurs. In Michael Gerber's bestselling book *The E-Myth Revisited*, he discusses that in essence all successful individual entrepreneurs possess each of these three traits in varying degrees and at different times. But although the business success depends on an owner having all these traits, the best choice in targeting a buyer usually comes down to the business situation, stage of maturity and size.

Technicians are good target buyers when the business requires a new owner to replace the technical work of the business being performed by the current owner. Technicians are often targeted for the smallest businesses. As we'll see later, valuation is improved when the business can carry on without the day-to-day attention of the owner. But many small businesses have not reached a size to have enough employees to do work that the owner does, or perhaps the various skills required. In these situations often the only option is for the seller to find someone with the requisite technical skills to perform the critical work creating and delivering the products or services sold.

Bill's drywall business consists of Bill and two employees. Known for his high quality, and reliable service, Bill's business has provided sufficient income for him to raise his three children and to allow him and his wife a comfortable lifestyle. Bill's employees are experienced, but Bill's presence is usually required on many jobs. So in order for the business to carry on successfully when Bill retires, Bill is seeking a buyer who has drywall industry experience with the financial ability to buy him out and the desire to have their own business. In other words, a Technician.

Technicians can be found by looking at competitors or similar businesses in other territories. Usually there is someone already in the business who might be interested in expanding their geography or their customer reach. Technicians can also be found among employees of either the seller's company or competitors.

Managers make good target buyers when the work of the business requires that the team and processes are coordinated and structured to deliver a great customer experience through efficiency and quality. The owner may not be critical to performing the work of the business, but is critical to developing the systems that help the business be consistent and profitable.

Kathy's salon has an enviable reputation in her community. Kathy employs or sub-contracts with 17 stylists who perform the work of the business providing haircuts, styling, coloring, manicures and pedicures. Kathy no longer does any of that work, but her efforts are focused on hiring, scheduling, marketing, inventory and finance. Kathy knows that many stylists don't have the desire or training to manage a business like hers. The buyer she seeks for her business is therefore not necessarily experienced in this industry. Her targeted buyer is a Manager, someone who has coordinated a team of employees, understands financial needs of a business and can carry on the marketing work she has established. Managers are often individuals who have been in a corporate or team environment where they've gained these skills and confidence. They realize that an investment in their own business doesn't require that they know the work of the business, and they are drawn to a business where their management skills can continue and even improve the profitability of the firm. Thus, they are able to forecast that their investment in the business will generate an acceptable financial return.

Entrepreneurs are buyers who possess a future vision of the business beyond what the selling owner has built or even imagines themselves. Entrepreneurs may be driven by the desire to build an "empire" off of the foundation of the business. Perhaps they see the business as having a tremendous growth potential that they can achieve because of its unique industry, product or service. Entrepreneurs may simply be financial investors who see the business as a way to harvest substantial financial return on their ownership investment.

Michael's water filtration business has established a strong market share through high service and quality levels, as well as by coverage of both consumer and industrial water filtration needs. Michael's team has developed a way to dramatically decrease the cost of large purifiers that has the potential to provide cleaner drinking water for many parts of the world. But they lack the knowledge and financial strength to expand into international markets, and Michael himself is starting to focus on his retirement years, rather than taking on a new business challenge. Michael seeks a buyer for his business who is excited to take on the financial risk of both continuing the success of the base business and, at the same time, charting a course to take the business into a high growth international market scene... an Entrepreneur.

Entrepreneurs often have strong networks among other business owners as well as bankers, attorneys, financial planners and others who are aware of opportunities like Michael's and can provide counsel on risk, financing, team building, and more. An Entrepreneur buyer may not come from the industry of the seller, but does likely possess the same interest in the broad purpose or mission of the business. A seller who wishes their business to carry on a legacy based on what they have built may want to attract an Entrepreneur who shares their vision of what the business could become.

FINANCIAL BUYERS

Recent years have seen a growth in financial buyers. Often identified under the labels of "investment buyers" or "private equity buyers", they are usually individuals or groups of investors who are seeking a higher return on their investment than may be found in other investment vehicles, or seeking to simply diversify their investments in a way where they may have more control over the results. Financial buyers tend to be less emotionally driven than individuals or even strategic buyers. They are more analytical about the past results of the business and more importantly, about its future prospects. Culture and legacy of the business are less important to a financial buyer unless they are strongly linked to its success. They may seek to retain existing key management people of the business to assure that the business has a strong chance of achieving at least the same level of results in the future as it did in the past. Sellability factors that will be discussed later in the book are important to all buyers, but are closely analyzed by financial buyers in calculating the business' valuation.

STRATEGIC BUYERS

Strategic buyers may be the most valuable, highly sought after target to acquire your business. They can be individuals, but are usually other companies who are looking to enhance the value of their own business through the acquisition of yours. Strategic acquisitions can be made for several reasons:

- Add value to an existing product or service of the buyer by "bolting on" the seller's product to add to its overall appeal or price.
- Add a separate product line or revenue stream that the buyer's existing customers would value.
- Increase market share by adding customer base or geography to the buyer's firm.
- Scale the business vertically. For example, the seller may be a key supplier to the buyer that would lower the overall cost of the buyer's products if both were under the same ownership.
- Acquire valuable technology, skill sets, patents, software or even employees that would enhance the buying firm's market position.

For a strategic buyer, there is more at stake than the financial return or emotional desire to own a given business. There is the health, strategic direction and future of the buyer's core business. For that reason, strategic buyers typically are willing to pay premium prices for strategic acquisitions. Strategic buyers can often be found by looking at competitors, customers and suppliers. A strategic buyer may also be in a related industry and looking to broaden their scope.

Megan's company manufactured food warming equipment and became a successful supplier to large chain restaurants as well as food equipment dealers across the country. The business was financially sound and Megan had built a comfortable lifestyle supported by the wealth and equity the company generated for her over the years. Megan's team worked well together and Megan felt that her VP of Sales, in particular, was capable of running the day-to-day operations of the business. Megan felt ready to take her life in a different direction, and put together an exit strategy team to find a buyer.

Two potential suitors emerged. One, an equity investment firm with a wide range of holdings in various industries, was attracted by the steady and growing earnings of the business as well as the management team. They carefully calculated that their $4.2 million offer would likely generate a payback within three and a half years, and a return on investment rate of at least 16%. Megan considered this a good and fair offer from, in essence, a financial buyer.

The other interested buyer also liked the financial performance of the business, but in addition saw the food warming equipment product line as an extension of their own line of commercial ovens and grills that were marketed through virtually the same distribution channels. Plus, Megan's company had a warehouse in a part of the country that would benefit the buyer by lowering shipping costs. Based on their projection of all the benefits of combining the two businesses, this strategic buyer offered Megan $5.3 million for the business. In addition to this attractive price, Megan liked the culture fit of this buyer, accepted their offer and closed the deal two months later.

As you may have already realized, buyers can be a blend of these three basic types. But it's important to consider the differences as you define the ideal target buyers for your business, as you develop your marketing message, and as you determine business valuation. When it comes to negotiating the sale price and terms, knowing the typical motivations of the buyer can help structure a deal that is a win-win for both parties.

Chapter 3 - Valuation – The Numbers

How much is your business worth? Can you recover the investments you've made over the life of the business? Will anyone else perceive the value in your business that you do? How do you set a price on your business that maximizes your return yet balances the desirability of the business to the right buyer?

These are critical questions. Thus one of the first steps in the process of selling a business is often to complete a valuation. Now before we go too far into this topic, it's important to make a strong point about valuation. **Ultimately the value of a business comes down to what the seller is willing to accept and what the buyer is willing to pay.** That means the price of the business is normally arrived at through a combination of justification and negotiation. The problem with many valuations is, they are mathematical formulas that may not reflect what the negotiated price will actually be. We'll discuss some non-mathematical drivers of value in the next chapter, and it's important to remember that these exist and do influence ultimate price.

Nonetheless, valuation of a business early in the selling process does have benefit. First of all, it may impact the seller's expectation of price. Paul owns a car wash business in a great location. It has seven washing bays, requires few employees to operate and has had a good track record of profitability. Over the years, Paul's friends have told him, "you have a million-dollar business" so many times that he has come to believe it. But a valuation of the business seems to indicate that its actual value is closer to $600,000. Without the valuation to initially buffer Paul's expectations, he runs the risk of never quite finding a buyer who feels they can realize a fair return on their investment.

Valuations also help start a discussion of what the seller can do to improve valuation prior to sale. Many buyers wake up one day, and say that it's time to sell as discussed in Chapter 1. But of course, if your goal is to maximize your sale value, it's wise to start much earlier in building the kind of business that will be attractive and fetch a premium price. Analyzing a valuation can lead to improvements in the business that increase price when it comes time for the sale. Joan's business was a successful manufacturer of upscale women's handbags. With higher price points and an affluent market, Joan's business was able to enjoy healthy profit levels over the past 10 years. However, in closely analyzing Joan's valuation, it showed that she typically carried much more inventory than her sales level would indicate. By working to bring inventory levels to a more competitive level, Joan not only turned the stock into immediate cash, but she also improved the ongoing cash flow of the business, which raised her valuation. Her inventory ratio then impressed the ultimate buyer as an indicator of the management strength of the company.

Finally, valuations are useful to educate both the seller and buyer about how or why a certain valuation is realistic. As such, it can be helpful in smoothing the negotiation and bringing the parties together on an acceptable final price. Four basic methods of calculating value are worth knowing, realizing that other methods also may come into play. It's useful to actually calculate your business value using all four of the methods, because the four different numbers tend to force us into considering a range of value rather than a single number. Often, one of the methods produce a number that is clearly an outlier and can be ignored. As you'll see, qualities of the business often determine which method(s) might indicate the closest level of true value.

VALUATION METHODS

Value of Sales

In some industries (for example, restaurants) businesses are sometimes valued at or near its level of annual sales. It is easy to calculate and readily understandable. This method may be appropriate when the "asset" that is sold primarily consists of the customer list, the brand, or the reputation. Value of Sales method makes sense when the ongoing revenue performance of the business seems likely to be as good as past performance. However, the shortcoming in use of this method alone is when sales trends don't accurately reflect profit trends for the business. Thus for a buyer seeking to calculate a return or a cash flow from the business purchase, more analysis is needed.

Value of Assets

This method is also somewhat easy to calculate as a starting point. Value of Assets may refer to receivables, inventory, equipment or fixed property and more. Current assets like receivables and inventory generally have a book value that accurately reflects actual value. Often, value of these assets is modified to reflect agreed realized value, i.e. if not all receivables are collectible, perhaps 80% (or other percentage) of book value is used. Or if some inventory is old or obsolete, another percentage of book value is agreed to, or an audit is performed. But typically, Value of Assets is used in heavy equipment industries or where significant and income producing property makes up the business. With fixed assets, their book value may not reflect the true present and ongoing value. In those cases, some type of assessed value or replacement value may be used.

Discounted Cash Flow

This method usually relies on performance trends, or on an agreed projection to calculate the present value of future cash flow of the business. From the standpoint of a financially oriented buyer, this method is the best indicator of what type of return on investment can be achieved. However, there are two key elements that need agreement between buyer and seller that can be difficult to pin down. First is the accuracy and likelihood of achieving the projected performance. Second is the length of time to include in the present value calculation (how many years of future projection to include).

End of Year	Pre-Tax Profit	**Present Value -15% Discount**	Accumulated Value
1	$100,000	$86,957	$86,957
2	$100,000	$75,614	$162,571
3	$100,000	$65,752	$228,323
4	$100,000	$57,175	$285,498
5	$100,000	$49,718	**$335,216**
6	$100,000	$43,233	$378,449
7	$100,000	$37,594	$416,043

In the above table, we see that the present value of an expected $100,000 of pre-tax profit in the coming year is worth $86,957 today, assuming it earns 15% year-to-year (the "discount rate," noted in the next paragraph). The second year at the same pre-tax profit level is discounted twice (two years) and is worth a little less today. The accumulation of these present value profits gives us an idea of valuation, but depends on the length of time a buyer is willing to wait for a return on his investment. As you can see, if a buyer accepts a 5-year return, he is willing to pay $335,216 for a business that has annual pre-tax profit of $100,000. In Discounted Cash Flow there is a strong element of reliance on the future projected earnings of the business. Will this business reliably earn $100,000 of profits each year? The further out one looks, the fuzzier the picture often becomes.

The other critical factor in this calculation is the assumed discount rate. A typical way of looking at discount rate is to consider what type of return can be achieved by other income producing investments. However, in a business investment, the riskier the business is perceived, the higher the investment rate the buyer will want to use, thus decreasing the present value numbers.

Because the Discounted Cash Flow method relies on projected financial results, it is a good method to use in a growth business because it recognizes future value of that growth. The best way to illustrate this is to look at the same example above, but with a 10% growth in annual pre-tax profit:

End of Year	Pre-Tax Profit	Present Value -15% Discount	Accumulated Value
1	$100,000	$86,957	$86,957
2	$110,000	$83,176	$170,133
3	$121,000	$79,559	$249,692
4	$133,100	$76,100	$325,792
5	$146,410	$72,792	**$398,584**
6	$161,051	$69,627	$468,211
7	$177,156	$66,599	$534,810

Clearly, the modest growth of the business in this example yields a 5-year discounted value of $398,584, which is an 18.9% improvement over the valuation of the same business with a flat projection of future profits in our first example.

Multiple of EBITDA

The most common valuation method used is Multiple of EBITDA. The acronym stands for "Earnings Before Interest, Taxes, Depreciation & Amortization". As such, it reflects the past or current performance of the business in terms of cash flow from operations, and is relatively easy to calculate. Business value is ultimately agreed on, based on a multiple of EBITDA. For example, you may hear the phrase "three times EBITDA" or "four times EBITDA". The multiple is indicative of the period of time (in years) that the buyer expects their investment to be recovered. Multiples typically range from 2 to 7, with 3 or 4 being most common. Larger businesses normally command higher multiples. The challenges with use of EBITDA are primarily in agreeing to the appropriate multiple and in understanding that it does not necessarily indicate future performance.

EBITDA indicates the amount of cash a business produces. Depreciation and amortization use no cash and therefore can be added back into profit to indicate actual cash produced. Interest and taxes are also added back because, although they are uses of cash, they may be very different amounts under new ownership. So a business with $100,000 of pre-tax net income, $7,000 of depreciation and $3,000 of interest would have EBITDA of $110,000.

Because EBITDA relies on past performance, one question that arises is how far into the past should buyers and sellers look to determine value? If profits are variable, jumping up and down over past years, it may be helpful to take an average of several past years' performance. If profits are growing, only the most recent one or two years will be enough to indicate value. Most people believe recent performance is the best indicator of what is to come, so the most recent year or two is given more weight in any averaging of performance. This can be done mathematically by assigning a numerical weighting as shown below:

Year Ended	EBITDA	% Weighting	Contributed Value
Dec. 2013	$100,000	40%	$40,000
Dec. 2012	$90,000	30%	$27,000
Dec. 2011	$125,000	20%	$25,000
Dec. 2010	$110,000	10%	$11,000
	Total Weighted Average EBITDA		**$103,000**

In the above example, although profits fell in the most recent two years compared to the prior two, the higher years still contributed to an EBITDA that resulted in a slightly higher value than the most recent year alone.

OTHER CONSIDERATIONS

Owner compensation

One important adjustment to consider in defining earnings (and EBITDA) is owner compensation. In a very small business, a buyer who is going to work in the business just as the prior owner did, may view the pay or draw taken by the prior owner as part of the financial return of the business. But if the buyer does not plan to work in the business themselves and intends to elevate staff or hire a manager, they may have to pay the staff or manager a similar compensation to what the seller takes. In the first example, the expense of owner compensation can be removed from the earnings calculation to show a higher (but actual) return to the buyer. But in the second example, owner compensation should remain part of the calculation to give the buyer an appropriate net earnings expectation.

Note that depending on the form of business incorporation, owners' compensation may or may not be part of earnings shown on an income statement. Typically businesses that are LLCs show owners' compensation outside of the income statement while C-corp businesses show compensation as salary on the income statement. Depending on the level of compensation, or its "reasonableness" or fair market value, over- or under-compensated adjustments may also be made.

Other forms of owners' compensation may also need to be adjusted to show buyers what the business truly looks like without the seller's involvement. One of the most common of these is rent. Often the building housing the business is owned by the seller and incorporated in a separate business. If the seller is not selling the building, the business may continue to operate there after sale, with rent continuing to be paid to the building owner. However, if the buyer plans to move the business, or perhaps merge it into another existing business, rent may be unnecessary to the buyer, and adjusting it from the earnings calculation will result in a higher value. Rent expense may also be adjusted to reflect fair market value if the current owner pays himself rent at a lower or higher level than the market might indicate.

Other owner compensation that should be adjusted on earnings statements include things like life or health insurance, mileage and vehicles, or any personal perks or privileges that will not continue or accrue to a seller.

Assets that transfer... or not
Regardless of the method of business valuation used, adjustments are often made based on assets that may or may not be transferred with the business (aka Excluded Assets). As mentioned above, a seller may want to retain a vehicle that is on the books of the business and an adjustment may be necessary to reflect that. But the bigger picture items that cause negotiating headaches are receivables and inventory.

On the surface, it seems as though the value of receivables is their face value. But, buyers may worry that upon transfer of ownership, some customers may renege on payment. They may also view suspiciously any receivables that are long overdue or have concern that collection may cause them grief due to tension or a dispute. As a result, buyers may want to discount the value of receivables. Sellers on the other hand, usually have a high degree of confidence in the collectability of receivables. They have the experience of knowing payment history of customers and may be able to leverage their past relationship to collect overdue accounts. So, sellers may retain receivables that occur prior to sale to maximize the total cash they collect in the business sale process. However, there is a down side to retaining receivables in some cases, and that is discussed in Chapter 4 in a section on "Valuation Teeter-Totter". Essentially, a buyer who can't count on the cash flow from receivables during the first months of their ownership may need to inject more working capital into the business and will feel that overall value should be decreased.

The other asset that may require value adjustment is inventory. With inventory, it is not just a question of who should own it, but rather, what it is worth. Almost all businesses have some amount of old, obsolete, slow-moving, dust-covered inventory. Even though inventory may be critical to producing revenue for the business, the questions revolve around how salable it is, and at what price. Book value of inventory is often discounted, sometimes as much as 50% or more due to this value question.

The other question about inventory is, of course, how much of it exists at time of sale. It is not usually practical to conduct a physical inventory on the day of sale, and because business is ongoing, determining the exact valuation of inventory is suspect. So buyers and sellers need to agree upon a method or formula to assess inventory value, and this negotiation can, at times, be a source of irritation in the sale process.

Valuation of a business, by the numbers, can be as much art as science. But the numbers matter! One of the most important ways that small businesses stumble in valuation is that they don't have complete and accurate financial records in the first place. Some business owners rely on their tax statements as a reflection of their business performance. Although tax records are better than nothing, think about the philosophy behind tax records versus operating financial statements. Taxes are typically prepared to take advantage of deductions and legitimate opportunities to <u>reduce</u> reported income. Why would a seller want to show reduced income, and thus, value? Operating financial statements are perceived by buyers to be more reflective of what is truly the earnings and value of a business.

At the same time, valuations that rely on projections or forecasts (like Discounted Cash Flow) can also be more art than science. After all, no one can truly predict the future, can they? So financial projections deserve thought and justification for the assumptions behind the numbers. Knowing the basis for the forecasts is an important factor in helping the seller push the final purchase price higher should a negotiation take place.

An accountant can and should validate the financial records to increase their credibility factor for the buyer. Remember that it is always recommended that an accountant or other professional experienced in valuation be consulted in any buy/sell situation.

Chapter 4 - Valuation – Sellability

"Sellability" was coined by John Warrillow, author of *"Built to Sell"*. John's book presents the story of a business owner who works with an advisor to build a business that becomes quite attractive to buyers and more valuable to the owner, than it would have been on its initial course. John has also created an immensely helpful way to measure a Sellability Score for business owners to measure the relative value or appeal of their business to a buyer. The higher the score, the greater the potential premium a buyer may pay for the business. If you are curious about your own business' Sellability Score, please take 15 minutes and complete a survey at http://baltusgroup.advicoach.com/sellability.aspx. You'll also receive an offer to meet with us at no charge to assess your score and your business improvement strategies.

John Warrillow's excellent algorithm used in calculating the Sellability Score is based primarily on eight important factors:

- Hub & Spoke
- Customer Satisfaction
- Monopoly Control
- Recurring Revenue

- Valuation Teeter-Totter
- Switzerland Structure
- Growth Potential
- Financial Performance

We have found that using the eight factors as marketing "talking points" with potential buyers can have a positive effect on the perceived valuation, regardless of the mathematical valuations described in Chapter 3. Including the most positive factors in the business' offering Prospectus (Chapter 5) creates a desirable marketing proposition.

But more importantly, the eight factors create a value improvement plan for business owners and their advisors. Having a low Sellability Score overall, or in specific factors, gives owners a place to start in improving the business. Similar to selling a house, if a seller learns that the home's roof is the weakest factor in creating a more valuable offer price, then working to improve or replace the roof is the obvious way to fetch a higher offer. In business, starting early to work on the weakest Sellability factors can pay immense dividends at time of sale. Let's examine these key factors that contribute to buyer attraction and greater value.

Hub & Spoke

Does your business revolve around you? Do you have trouble trusting the critical operations of your business to your employees? Are you able to step away from your business for more than a few days to enjoy the rest of your life, or do you consider that too risky? The answers to these questions may indicate that you are such a strong "hub" around which your entire business revolves, that without you, it cannot continue to spin.

Even if your business is successful in many other aspects, any buyer who senses that without your presence, the business may not operate as successfully as it has in the past, will not be willing to invest as much in it. If you are the Hub and are indispensable to do the "technical" work of your business, then only similar "technical" buyers will likely be interested in the business.

Consider the following antidotes to an owner Hub:

- A secondary leader who has the skill and acumen to run the critical aspects of the business. Buyers will rely on this secondary leader to help them continue the financial performance after your departure.
- A strong team who work well together and share the operation of the critical functions of the business, but may require an owner with the strategic vision to continue evolving the business in reaction to market trends and customer needs.
- You, the owner, being able to consistently delegate work among your team, so that you are able to step away with confidence that the business can continue to operate successfully.

Customer Satisfaction

Nearly all business owners tell us that they achieve high levels of customer satisfaction. But in terms of the attractiveness of your business, the key to the value of your customer satisfaction is the ability of the business to prove it.

Think about it... Your customers love you, right? After all, customers seldom complain. Oh sure, you get the occasional irate phone call, but who doesn't? You do good work, so who wouldn't be satisfied? You have this customer satisfaction factor in the bag, and should be able to fetch a premium price for your business because of it, right?

We as business owners are often too close to the technical work of the business to assess the level of customer satisfaction that exists. We tend to have a "no news is good news" mentality. But to a savvy buyer, that attitude indicates a business with a customer satisfaction level that is average at best. So we need to have both high customer satisfaction and proof of it.

The essence of customer satisfaction is delivering on your brand promise. It is having a great product or service and having an attitude and delivery system for your business that sets you apart from your competitors and compels people to do business with you. Excellence in every facet of your business is the most important path to customer satisfaction, and it often requires a continuous improvement culture that keeps competitors at bay. Operational excellence is how true "word of mouth" marketing is achieved.

But it is proof of customer satisfaction that we want to focus on, in terms of the attractiveness of your business. One method presented in Sellability Score analysis is Net Promoter Score. Net Promoter is based on surveying customers about how likely (on a 1 – 10 scale) they are to refer your business to someone else. Auto dealers and insurance companies (among many others) strive for scores of 9 or 10 to show that their customer service levels are high... better than competition. Net Promoter Score is an excellent way of proving customer satisfaction and of scoring your business's progress toward higher levels.

Implementing Net Promoter Score in your business may be the most ideal and widely accepted way to define your level of customer satisfaction, but are there other ways you could prove how good your business is? Do you routinely get referrals from customers? Could you track them? Better yet, could you encourage them? What kind of referral building program do you have in place? One client of mine simply uses a letter board in his lobby to list names of customers who have referred other customers to him. People love recognition and this becomes an inexpensive way to encourage referrals. Of course, my client needs to track referrals in order to give the recognition, so he has a built-in proof of customer satisfaction.

How about repeat customers? What kind of measure can you create that would tell prospective buyers that 93% of your customers keep coming back? That kind of proof of customer satisfaction is powerful.

Or, could you do a better job of asking for customer testimonials? If your business serves a relatively small number of customers, even a few testimonials can represent a large percentage of satisfied customers. Testimonials not only prove customer satisfaction, they are also an important marketing tool that can enhance your entire marketing plan and lead to greater revenue.

What other ways can you create to prove that your business excels at satisfying customers?

Note: Net Promoter Score is a trademark of Satmetrix Systems, Inc., Bain & Company, Inc., and Fred Reichheld.

<u>Monopoly Control</u>
Wouldn't it be great if you had no competitors? Your
market share would be 100% and you could avoid ever
having to discount prices. You wouldn't abuse such power,
no, not you! But you'd enjoy profits that would support
your team and your life so that you could live the dream.

Well, we all know that free market capitalism actually
works better than monopolies at creating better products
and service and that competition raises the bar in all areas
of business. Nonetheless, monopoly (or close to it) is
attractive because it infers higher profits. Buyers like
profits, so the closer your business is to having "Monopoly
Control", the more buyers are attracted. In free-market
capitalism, if you create an attractive new product or
service that no one else has, you will enjoy monopoly, but
usually not for very long. Other entrepreneurs will copy or
even improve on what you have and competition will
ensue. So how do you develop a level of monopoly control
that enhances the value of your business in the eyes of
potential buyers?

Apart from actually possessing a unique product or service,
the next best thing is possessing the <u>perception</u> that your
business is unique and special. In marketing, perception is
reality, as we all know. Why do drug companies spend
billions of dollars on marketing campaigns that
differentiate their product from other branded or generic
forms of the same prescription? It is largely to enhance the
perception that they have the better, more trusted product
and thus improve their market share.

To enhance the perception (and market share) of your
business, think about what makes your business unique,
what sets you apart? Could you promote and focus on an

element of your business that you do best? Do you know
what your current customers care most about that keeps
them coming back? Is there a layer of service that you
could improve upon to create a "Wow" factor that gets
customers talking? Can you define your market share, even
in an approximate way, that would help a buyer sense your
monopoly control?

Bruce's law firm worked with clients in a wide variety of
legal areas, from business to insurance to property to
divorce and more. But Bruce and his team seemed to
attract more clients in the area of Estates, Wills and Trusts
than any other area. By working on developing even
greater expertise in this area and by creating simple tools to
expedite results for clients, they were able to create a
reputation of being the "go-to" law firm for this work, and
their market share steadily increased. Did they have a
monopoly? No, but they created a perception of being the
best in this focused area of law, and it gave them an
element of monopoly control.

Without a unique selling proposition, without a brand
promise that draws customers and without truly unique
products or services, a business is in commoditization.
Commodity-level competition reduces business to
competing solely on price, and for most of us that is a
losing proposition and a detractor from business value.

Recurring Revenue
Not every business can enjoy recurring, ongoing revenue
streams, but if you have strong recurring, repeat revenue
and customers, you have a more attractive business. One of
the most critical questions a buyer has, is whether the past
financial success of the business will continue under their

ownership. And although most buyers have a certain egotistical element to their motivation, i.e. that they will be able to outperform the previous owner, there is always a fear about how sales will continue to flow.

So recurring revenue is a blessing, a relief even, to most buyers. It provides a base from which their efforts can springboard to even higher levels. It creates a level of certainty that past performance will determine future results. What kind of recurring revenue does your business have? What could you do to build more recurring revenue? Here are some types you may recognize:

- Service contracts – How great is it to charge monthly or annually under a contract that continues over several years (think cell phone companies)?
- Subscriptions – Is there a service or product your business provides that permits customers to subscribe so that they receive that item year after year?
- Consumables – If you sell a product that is repetitively used in support of a larger, fixed product, it may be that customers need to continue buying those items from you for years.
- Customer loyalty programs – The prevalence of frequent customer cards, clubs and benefits help to drive repeat business in industries from airlines to restaurants to credit cards and beyond.

Here, as in our discussion above about customer satisfaction, proof of recurring revenue is going to be important to buyers. What percentage of your revenue recurs year after year? What is your customer turnover? Keeping records of these kinds of measurements will pay off when it comes to convincing a buyer that they should

pay a little more for your business because your revenue
stream is secure.

Valuation Teeter-Totter

If you purchase a home, but realize that you'll need to
replace the windows shortly after purchase, how does that
affect your view of the value of that home? It decreases it,
doesn't it?

Valuation Teeter-Totter works in much the same way. If the
buyer perceives that they will need to inject working capital
into the business after purchase, it is going to negatively
affect the amount they will invest in the business. So
creating a business that has strong ability to accumulate
cash as it grows, or immediately upon sale, is a more
valuable business.

An interesting way to consider Valuation Teeter-Totter is to
look at what happens with Accounts Receivable in a
business sale transaction. As mentioned in Chapter 3,
buyers often question the collectability of receivables and
want to discount their value. They may feel that upon
ownership change, some customers will abandon their
obligations, or if the company has experienced bad debts in
the past, it may be briefly worsened upon sale. The seller,
on the other hand, usually feels secure in the collectability
of the receivables and so the sale transaction is structured
so that the seller owns the receivables that exist at date of
sale. That means that the buyer starts out the first day of
ownership with no receivables and thus no incoming cash
until new sales and payment cycles kick in. So the buyer
has to consider how they will fund working capital in the
first days of the business, thus potentially lowering what
they are willing to pay for the business.

Improving your Valuation Teeter-Totter factor revolves around good cash flow management, particularly shortening the business's "cash gap". The cash gap is the time difference between when you get paid and when you have to pay for goods or services you sell. Often we have to pay for what we sell (our cost of goods payments) before we get paid. So to shorten our cash gap we have to consider how to speed up our collections of receivables or lengthen our time for paying vendors. Speeding up collections can be done by decreasing terms, offering payment discounts, receiving down payments or use of credit card collections. Lengthening of vendor payments should be done with discretion so as not to harm vendor relationships. Service businesses where labor cost is the primary cost of sale have difficulty pushing out payments for cost since this is primarily a payroll issue.

Nonetheless, good management of the cash gap is an important factor in reducing the working capital needed by a buyer, and that improves business value.

Switzerland Structure
When most people think of Switzerland, they think of it as a neutral country. In its history, Switzerland has not taken sides, has not been drawn into war or skirmishes and has not been beholden to other countries. As a result, Switzerland has largely escaped from losses in capital or human life.

In terms of business value, we use the Switzerland factor to determine how beholden the company is to influences that might cause it harm. The most common issue here is the influence that one or a few customers might have on the business. If one customer has significant contribution to the revenue of the business, loss of that customer could severely diminish the ability of the company to remain as profitable as the buyer expected. So buyers will look critically on customers that contribute significantly, say 20-25% or more, to the revenue base.

Craig owned a small business making food warmers, and employed 10 people. Good fortune came their way one year when Craig landed a big box retailer who purchased one of Craig's models to stock their shelves on stores nationwide. The first food warmer was a hit and the big box store expanded their purchases to other models as well. Craig's business exploded. His employee base jumped to 53, he moved the business to a larger facility and life was good. The big box retailer grew to 80% of Craig's business. His friends, vendors, bank and others warned him that his business was vulnerable, but although he knew it, he couldn't find the time to expand his customer base nor the courage to scale back his product line to the big box retailer. After five years of tremendous success, the retailer dropped Craig's line in favor of another vendor. Craig couldn't cut costs fast enough and within six months was out of business.

Had Craig tried to sell his business at its height, how do you think the value would have been perceived? Although the business was strong in cash flow for the moment, it would have been obvious to a buyer that their investment would have carried a high risk. Its Switzerland Structure was very low.

Similar to customer concentration, businesses can also have a low Switzerland factor by being dependent on a key supplier or even a key employee. So in building a more valuable business, it is important to look at all dependencies in your business and find ways to decrease dependency so that loss of a key component has minimal effect on profit and cash creation.

Growth Potential
You've built a great business that has served your life over the years and now are ready to cash out. You've reached a stage in your life where your energy level isn't what it used to be, so you haven't worked too hard to continue growing the business. But you see the potential. If you were younger (you tell yourself), you would expand into the neighboring state. You would add a complementary product line that a number of customers have asked about. You'd probably invest in that new robotic laser cutter/welder machine you've been hearing about.

The key is, your business has potential! Buyers are confident, even slightly arrogant. They believe in themselves and their ability to improve upon the business they are purchasing. But if they see that the current owner believes in the potential of the business as well, it's a double-jackpot bonus.

For that reason, it's important to lay out your ideas for the growth potential of your firm. And the best way to do that is to complete a Strategic Plan. When a strategic plan is suggested to a seller, they usually dismiss the idea initially. They don't have the intention of carrying it out, so why bother? They feel they've gotten by thus far without one, so why spend time and money now? But having a strategic plan, believing in it and being able to confidently and coherently explain it, is incredibly valuable in a business sale. Not only that, but because the sale process can seem long, often taking months or even years to complete, a strategic plan can give the business some focus, something to work on so that the business and ownership doesn't fall into "coast mode".

Financial Performance
The eight Sellability factors have been presented here in order of their significance in the Sellability Score algorithm, from lowest to highest. As you might imagine, Financial Performance carries the highest weight, in determining the attractiveness value of a business. But similar to some of the other factors we've discussed, Financial Performance is only useful if you can prove it. So one of the areas many small businesses can improve upon is their financial recordkeeping.

Shawn's excavation business had its' ups and downs in the 24 years that Shawn owned it. It was modestly profitable, had a number of reliable contractors from whom it regularly received referrals and had relatively new and modern equipment as an asset base. Shawn knew his financial condition pretty well, but relied on his checkbook to tell him how he was doing, and didn't really understand income statements and balance sheets. His bookkeeper had become lax in her efforts to get the financial details recorded correctly in recent years, and Shawn's accountant simply took care of the tax requirements as best he could. When Shawn's banker reviewed his line of credit every year he asked for a set of financial statements, but didn't examine them too closely as they were primarily for the file. Besides, Shawn was always conscientious about paying his loans and was a trusted bank client.

When it came time to sell the business, Shawn had a couple of interested buyers. But as they and their accountants reviewed the financials of Shawn's business they noticed discrepancies and inconsistencies that were hard to explain. Shawn's cost of sales ratios were higher than the industry average, but the numbers seemed to bounce up and down each year. Accounts receivable aging reports showed some old receivables which actually had been paid months ago. A backhoe sold two years earlier was still listed on the asset list and it was discovered that its sale was booked to operating revenue, which inflated sales in that year. All of these discrepancies resulted in low buyer confidence of the financial condition for the business, and buyer interest in the business disappeared.

Income statements (or Profit & Loss statements) and Balance Sheets are basic financial tools that are commonly understood. When a business deviates from their use or fails to pay attention to their accuracy or does not keep them current, it diminishes the business value. Thus to prepare your business for the day of its eventual sale or transfer, it is critical that you regularly review and understand your financial status.

IRONY OF SELLABILITY

Whether you are ready to sell your business immediately, or have time to work on improving its value, you will find the above eight Sellability factors useful. We have found that there is a beautiful irony (actually two ironies) that occurs as you work to improve your business attractiveness.

First, let's suppose you have reached a point in your life where the business just isn't as much fun anymore. You're feeling that you don't have the energy that you used to, and that it may be time to get serious about an exit strategy. Together with your business coach, you define a couple of key Sellability factors you'd like to improve over the next 12-24 months to maximize the business' sales value. The irony is that as improvements are implemented, you may find that the business starts to be more interesting and fun again. I've had clients tell me that they want to delay selling the business a little longer as their exit strategy evolves. The reason that happens is that the business may be generating more cash (profits), or a key employee or the entire team may be functioning better, thus needing less of your day-to-day attention in order to succeed. Your life becomes easier, more stress-free, and you decide to work on growing even greater equity in your business asset.

The other irony happens to business owners who are nowhere near the stage of selling their business. Maybe they've been in business 5-15 years, are feeling good about what they've built, and are executing a plan to continue to improve equity value. (Remember that for most small business owners the business is often their primary retirement asset, so working on equity is like improving your stock portfolio.) Because the business then becomes more valuable, others notice (think competitors, suppliers, customers) and suddenly an inquiry appears about whether they'd like to sell. In spite of no intention to sell the business, their efforts have given them the chance to liquidate their current business earlier than anticipated and use the proceeds to invest in other retirement assets, plus start a second business that intrigues them.

Chapter 5 - Preparing for Sale

Marvin owned a lawn and garden equipment business selling lawn mowers, snow blowers, tillers, chain saws and the like. He had a good reputation, great location, well-known brands and a small but effective team that was able to flex with the seasonal nature of the business. Marvin also carried a large amount of debt, which he was able to manage in normal times. However, following a warm winter with little snow and then a warm, dry summer with little grass to mow, Marvin's business slowed to a standstill. But the debt payment demands continued, of course. Marvin's creditors chased payments more frequently, and the bank grew nervous. Eventually, Marvin felt that it was all causing more pressure than he could endure. Nervously he told his team that he didn't know how long he could hold out. A week later, his ace serviceman gave notice of leaving. In another week, he lost his primary salesman. Now the pressure built to the boiling point and Marvin decided to close the doors, return inventory to vendors and tell the bank he was done. The bank sold the business for roughly the value of the debt it was owed, and Marvin walked away with nothing to show for his years of effort.

Notwithstanding the stress Marvin endured, losing his employees and closing were expensive mistakes from the standpoint of maximizing a sales price for the business. Although the business was barely profitable following the warm winter and dry summer, he had a team, a customer base and dealerships that would have been valuable to a buyer. In the end, the decisions Marvin made, may have cost him $100,000.

Few business sales will take place under such duress. But the point of the story is that a successful business sale doesn't usually happen suddenly nor by serendipity. It happens on purpose and it happens due to careful preparation. Let's examine the variety of things that are necessary to prepare for a successful sale.

Mental Preparation & Attitude

For many sellers, nearing the stage of selling their business can be a relief. Once we've made a decision to take this path, the decision often changes our entire thought process and we begin to focus on the new vision of our future. For most of us, that can be a dangerous shift because of the tendency to take our focus off of our business. If we let the business drift during this time period, it may be evident to a potential buyer, and cause the sales price to diminish. So the mental challenge sellers need to take on, is that of working harder than ever to keep the business thriving and healthy.

One of the most difficult challenges sellers face is that selling a business usually happens only once in their lifetime. So in spite of knowing everything about running their successful business, this last major act of their professional career involves doing something they've never done before. How do we get started? Who can we trust? What if we screw it up? How long will it take? All of the unknowns are fear-producing (see Chapter 1) and on top of that, doing something new or different makes most of us uncomfortable. For many people, the predominant reaction to these challenges is to procrastinate. And that leads to waiting too long, or not being ultimately prepared to maximize the business value should a buyer appear.

To overcome the mental challenges that show up, it pays to set your mind on the goal and on the positive aspects of the process. You've likely overcome hundreds of obstacles during your business life, so you can certainly overcome one more. You can look forward to your vision of the next stage of your life with the attitude of leaving this stage a winner. You can envision a successful and happy sales process, and imagine your business thriving in the future under a new owner who is carrying on the legacy you've started. In short, it's critical to put yourself in a positive, forward-looking mindset, ready to take on the hard work of this last stage of business ownership.

Valuation

If you skipped Chapter 3 on Valuation because you thought it might be too boring or because you hate thinking about numbers, I urge you to muster your resolve to get through it and try again. In preparing yourself to sell your business, it's not enough to simply have a number in mind. It is important that you know why that number exists so that you can defend it and "sell" it. As mentioned in Chapter 3, valuations help to educate you, the seller, about the aspects of your business that are working well and those that aren't. Not only can it help you focus on where to make improvements, it can help you to emphasize the positives in discussions with potential buyers. Thus, a valuation can also be useful in educating a potential buyer.

Knowing the level of price you'd like to fetch for your business helps to motivate sellers to keep the business performance strong, and not start coasting toward retirement causing the business to go into decline. Very simply, having that valuation gives sellers a goal, and as we all know, goal-setting is critical to success for most of our activities in life.

Strategic Plan

Why in the world would someone who's eager to exit their business want to put time and effort into preparing a strategic plan? They aren't planning to be around to carry it out. The buyer will probably have their own ideas about what they want to do with the business. So why create a strategic plan?

Very simple. You as the seller know your business better than anybody. A buyer might want to know what you are thinking regarding the future possibilities for your business. Do you see decline and threats that are causing you to want to exit? Are there possibilities and opportunities that the business could pursue if you were going to stay on and lead your business to a better tomorrow? Buyers are obviously more inclined to pay more for businesses that have a bright future. The seller's perception of that future is an important selling point. You may be thinking that you don't care what the buyer does with the business; after all, it's theirs, not yours at that point. But is that really true? Most sellers have the desire to see their business continue with the reputation and direction they've established and even look for buyers with the same culture and values they have.

If your business has a team that will be part of the ongoing business, having that team aligned to the strategic direction of the business, is also a bonus. Strategic planning helps create that team alignment, especially if key team members have a hand in creating the strategic plan. That gives a buyer even more confidence that the business can continue to produce growth and profits.

Thinking through a strategic plan also helps put you, the seller, in a more forward-looking state of mind. The sale process doesn't usually go quickly. So having a couple key strategies or directions to work on in the meantime, actually helps tremendously to keep your attitude positive and focused.

Business Evaluation & Improvement
The very best approach to selling your business is to prepare ahead of time; ideally one to three years prior to an actual sale. It gives you time to create an accurate and appropriate financial picture, time to build a team (or at least a "second-in-command") who can cover the work you do in the business, and time to further systematize the business so that its processes are replicable and duplicable regardless of who is operating them. All of these preparation strategies lead to maximizing the equity you will harvest at time of sale.

Your business evaluation can take place in a variety of ways already described, including a financial valuation of the business, its Sellability Score and a strategic plan. Your advisers may use other tools to help evaluate the health of the business. But this is not where the work ends, in fact, this is where it begins. Creating a simple plan of the strategies you will work on during this preparation time is step one, and then working with your advisers to hold you and them accountable to putting the strategies in place is where the real value comes from.

Many owners forego this preparation, or business improvement stage and instead engage a business broker at the last moment to help market the business and seek a buyer. Or, if the firm is smaller than business brokers typically handle, the owners will try to sell it themselves or through their banker, real estate broker, attorney or other adviser. Although this can work, it will typically not generate the maximum value for the business, and could dramatically extend the timeframe of the actual sales process.

Gary had a terrific glass products business focused primarily on residential and commercial windows and doors. He had built a solid reputation, had well defined operating and financial processes and a track record of growth and profitability. But Gary was the primary driver; the "rain-maker"; the glue that held it all together. It wasn't that he didn't have capable people; he did! But he thrived in his hands-on leadership role, and never took the time to develop anyone on his team to take on more responsibility. In addition, Gary was the primary face of the business, and nearly all important sales relationships were his personally. Some of his most important customers had never spoken to anyone in the business other than Gary.

Gary's strategic plan and Sellability analysis revealed the weakness in the way the company was organized and in how Gary's leadership detracted from maximizing the value of the business. So Gary and his business coach created a plan to identify and develop two of his best people; one to focus on Operations and the other on Sales. The plan also required Gary and his team to add to his operations manual all the procedures that Gary himself followed, but never bothered to record. Most importantly, the Sales approach that made Gary's company successful, needed to be recorded, taught and practiced so that other team members could create revenue as well as Gary. The plan not only identified the tasks to be done, but the timeframe needed and the participants responsible, so that Gary's coach could help hold him and his team accountable to the progress they wanted and needed to make.

Prospectus

If you've ever purchased stocks or mutual funds, you have probably received a prospectus of the asset. Have you ever read it? I didn't think so. For most of us, they are good to read if we can't sleep at night! But these types of prospectus documents are required by law and are somewhat like the annual report of the company, only more legalistic in tone. They typically include the objectives and policies of the fund, risks and costs, management, past performance and operational issues. In short, it is meant to be an executive summary helping the investor to have a realistic overview of the asset so that they can make an informed decision or assess their risk before the purchase.

Your business prospectus is hopefully somewhat more interesting and appealing, but its purpose is not much different. You are looking to provide an executive overview of the business with enough details that an initial assessment of interest can be made by a prospective buyer. If well done, your prospectus can lead to a Letter of Intent (LOI), which starts the sale process. Normally, the prospectus doesn't produce a final offer, because it doesn't contain all of the details that a buyer may want to investigate before locking in on a price and terms of purchase. But short of going through an entire intricate due diligence process with every prospect (see Chapter 6), the prospectus allows a high level assessment of whether the business fits with the prospect's financial capability, risk tolerance, market type and other key decision factors.

Your business prospectus should be factual, but can typically include some statements and opinions of management outlook and judgment. Some of these may be related to the Sellability factors discussed in Chapter 4. For example, if you are in a growth market, you may be able to not only provide market statistics in your prospectus, but also your outlook for the growth of your business. If you have groomed a great "second-in-command" on your team, you may want to expand on the ability of the business to operate without the day-to-day, hands-on involvement of you, the owner.

There are many examples of business prospectus documents on the internet and in various related guides. The following simple outline of prospectus topics will give you an idea of the type of material which may be included:

- Executive Summary of Company (Industry, Years in business, Key markets)
- History
- Owner(s)
- Products / Services
- Market and Marketing Strategies
- Key Customers
- Culture
- Organization
- Competition

- Value (Price) and Sellability justification
- Financials – Historical and Projected (usually 3 to 5 years)
- List of Assets
- Strategic Position and Outlook
- On-site Photos and Map

Identifying Potential Buyers

As sellers, we often tend to think of a buyer as looking a lot like the image we see in the mirror. You think it will take someone just like you to own and run your business, because that's your paradigm of how the business has become successful (with you at the helm). As described in Chapter 2, however, you can start to get a sense that there may be several new avenues of business ownership that could take the business in a new direction you hadn't imagined as the owner.

One disadvantage that small business owners have (Ha!! Only ONE, you might ask?) is that business brokers typically work with businesses in the value range of about $1.5 million and above. So small business sellers don't usually have the benefit of finding someone with a network of buyers or a promotion vehicle like a Business-For-Sale board or website to help with their buyer search. Often it is the efforts of the owner and their advisers that identify and approach prospective buyers, or use their existing networks to put the word out about the new ownership and investment opportunity.

To begin identifying potential buyers and start to network around those that could put you in touch with them, it helps to answer the following questions as a way to build a prospect list:

- Who are your direct competitors?
- Who are your strategic partners and key suppliers?
- What companies in your industry have a large sales force (and could therefore absorb your product/service into their offering)?
- What companies could sell more of their product/service by adding your products/services to their offering?
- What companies could more easily compete against their competitors with the addition of your product/service?
- What companies might like to buy your business to expand geographically into locations that you serve?
- Who have you recruited employees from, or who has poached employees from you?
- Of all the companies listed in the questions above, which have the perceived revenue and financial wherewithal to make the investment in your business?

Once you have your prospective buyer list in hand, it's time to reach out and quietly inform them that your business is for sale, that you identified them as the kind of buyer that could carry on the legacy you've started, and assess their initial interest. It may be wise at this point to ask them to sign a Confidentiality/Non-Disclosure agreement to highlight the seriousness of the discussion and to assure the information they gain, will not be used against you or the eventual buyer.

Similarly, reach out to the bankers and accountants in your network to let them know of your intentions. Bankers and accountants are often approached by others interested in certain business investments because those people also lack a "marketplace" of small businesses for sale. Be open to network with others who may be aware of an interested party. Some of these include attorneys, sales reps who call on you, and certain customers or suppliers.

Lions and Tigers and Bears... Oh My!

In Chapter 1 on the emotions of selling, we discussed some of the issues surrounding the typical fears of the selling experience. This is a good time to touch on another important fear that nearly always affects the process. As sellers, we usually fear letting the word out that our business is for sale. We fear that business may drop off because customers may think we're closing. We fear employees will start seeking other jobs they perceive as more stable. At times, these fears are justified. Customers, employees, suppliers and others may be dealing with their own fears and uncertainties. And their fears might induce them to take actions that would be harmful to your business or to the selling process.

Essentially there are two basic paths to take in dealing with the rumors or uncertainties that crop up. One is to do everything possible to maintain confidentiality, even secrecy about the pending sale or process. The other is to be fairly open and honest with your intentions and the hoped-for outcome to dispel any misperceptions or rumors before they get started. Every sale situation will be different in regard to which approach (or combination thereof) will work best. But the primary determinant of which way to go probably depends most on you, the seller.

What are you most comfortable with? Can you really maintain a business-as-usual approach during the selling process that will not tip-off others? Can you button-up any discussions with advisers or buyer prospects that will assure their confidential treatment of the discussions? Would you be able to maintain secrecy in the event of a buyer tour of your facilities or during the due diligence phase discussed in Chapter 6?

On the other hand, how good are you at open, honest communication with employees that will assure them that their best interests are secure? Have you established customer and supplier understanding that they do business with your firm, not with you? Depending on the type of buyer sought for the business, what is the anticipated impact on each of these stakeholders, and how likely are they to help you achieve a successful outcome?

Both strategies take effort, planning and solid execution. Face it, if we've prepared properly up to this point, our staff, our customers and others are probably sensing that we're moving in this direction. The reality is, that everyone retires someday. If our message is clear and we're open regarding our intent and strategy, we often find that employees and customers actually rally to help us realize our dream and respect our direction.

Chapter 6 - Selling Process

Jake's Hauling had supported Jake and his family throughout the 40 years that he owned the business. He had earned enough money over the years to enjoy a fairly comfortable lifestyle... nothing extravagant, but enough to raise two healthy, smart kids who had grown into respectable adults and were leading lives of their own and raising their own families. Neither of Jake's children were interested in carrying on the trucking business. Jake and his wife, Ann, one day decided that it was time to retire. After a long talk over the weekend, Jake called his friendly competitor, Louis, who owned Lou's Trucking. They had worked side-by-side on a few large construction jobs over the years, and Jake knew Louis to be someone he could trust and whose thinking was similar to his about the right way to do things in the business. Lou's Trucking was larger than Jake's and also specialized in additional services like specialized piping excavation and heavy equipment transport. Jake told Louis about his retirement plans and asked Louis if he'd be interested in buying the business. Without hesitation, Louis explained that he had always thought that Jake's Hauling would make a perfect addition to his existing business because it offered additional equipment capacity and a customer list that would readily provide new cash flow. Louis called his banker to arrange a meeting the next day. On Tuesday, Jake met Louis at the bank and Louis transferred $1 million to Jake's account in payment for the business. The banker had arranged a bill of sale for the business, and upon signing it, Jake began his retirement, knowing that he and Ann were financially secure for their coming years.

Okay, as nice as that happy ending sounds, selling your business DOESN'T WORK THIS EASILY! Perhaps we could all agree that it SHOULD be that easy, but the reality is that there is more to it.

In Chapter 5, we looked at preparation for the sale of your business, and hopefully that preparation has yielded one or more prospective buyers who are at least interested in learning more details about your business. At this point, the selling process can occur via a number of routes, but typically we find that there are three "phases" that occur in most sales:

- Letter of Intent
- Due Diligence
- Purchase Agreement

Letter of Intent

Once a prospective buyer has been approached and they've expressed some interest in the business, asking them to review your prospectus is the best way to get the conversation started. The prospectus helps to answer many questions at arm's length as opposed to the seller and buyer actually having a verbal discussion about these details. This "arm's length" look at the prospectus helps to keep a discussion from turning into a price negotiation right away, and instead lets the merits of the business explain the price point desired. As a seller, it is to your benefit to have your business presented this way. Have you ever had a conversation where you walked away and thought of something clever that you should have said, but didn't think about at the time? That is the kind of scenario that the prospectus helps to avoid as most of the key aspects of the business will be explained via the document rather than by your memory.

If not done during your initial prospecting, prior to giving a potential buyer the prospectus, request that they sign a "confidentiality/non-disclosure agreement (NDA). As a seller, you would prefer that the details provided in the prospectus not become universally known, and the confidentiality/NDA agreement simply provides you with some level of security about this. It also reminds the buyer that you are serious about disclosing all the data they need to reach a decision, based on their assurance of keeping the details confidential. Serious buyers will have no problem executing a confidentiality/NDA agreement.

If your prospectus has convinced a prospect that your business is of interest, they may have some questions that have arisen from the prospectus, and further discussion and information may be exchanged. But at this stage, you don't know if the prospect is serious yet, so any exchange of information should be brief and essentially for the purpose of clarification. But this brings up a dilemma. How does an interested prospect make a firm offer to buy without knowing more details about the business that may be necessary for them to affirm that the business is right for them and that the asking price is appropriate? The answer is the "letter of intent" (LOI).

The LOI is a letter from the buyer to the seller which, as the name implies, defines the intent of the buyer to purchase the business. It can be brief or lengthy depending on how well-defined the buyer's intent is. At a minimum, it may contain a statement of the price the buyer is offering to pay, how the payment will be made, and the timing for the close of the transaction. It can also be nearly as complex as the purchase agreement, defining all or most of the terms that the purchase agreement will contain. (See purchase agreement section below.)

Normally, the buyer will draft the LOI with the help of their attorney. The LOI sets the stage for detailed terms of the purchase agreement, so attorneys are best suited to assist with this document. The LOI also may set some parameters for the "due diligence" process (See Due Diligence section below.)

But here is the strange and confusing thing about the LOI. It is not usually a 100% legally binding document! As the name implies it signals "intent," not commitment. In spite of the fact that it may contain a price point, terms, closing deadline, and more, the buyer still has not executed a binding purchase agreement. So you might ask, what good is it?

Well, it's a written instrument that expresses what the Buyer says he/she will do. Based on the facts available to them, which may be only those from the Prospectus, it is the best offer they can make at the time. But in order to finalize their offer, a buyer often will want to explore more details and assure themselves that all aspects of the transaction are suitable. That's what the due diligence period is for. You might ask, then why not go right into due diligence? The answer is that due diligence is a lot of work for both parties, as you'll see below. What if an interested prospect goes all the way through a due diligence period, but then simply says, "I've changed my mind. This looks like a good business, but I really don't want to buy it after all." What a waste of time that would be for the seller, and during that time, what other buyer prospects might have slipped past? The LOI provides strong assurance that the buyer will follow through with purchase if their due diligence confirms the value indicated in the Prospectus and reveals nothing negative that would alter their original intent.

Though rarely done, one way to strengthen the commitment value of the LOI is through the addition of an accompanying down payment, deposit or "earnest money." The buyer may offer an earnest money payment (to be fully or mostly returned if purchase does not take place), or the seller may request an earnest money payment as justification for the work of the due diligence period, depending upon how thorough that work is anticipated to be. A third party (usually bank or attorney) may be the holder of the earnest money payment during due diligence, and this payment will become part of the purchase price upon closing.

One additional aspect of note related to the LOI, is the possible inclusion of a clause requesting exclusivity during due diligence. Sometimes known as a "no shop" clause, the prospective buyer is simply asking that during this time of due diligence, the seller refrain from actively seeking other buyers or any negotiations with them. Sellers need to consider this clause based on how they perceive their chances of finding other buyers, the projected time period for due diligence, and their assessment of the seriousness of the buyer. Obviously if the seller finds themselves in the enviable position of possessing two or more LOIs, an exclusivity clause may not be viable nor acceptable.

Due Diligence
You've written a beautiful, thorough Prospectus that paints a terrifically attractive picture of your business. You've received a serious Letter of Intent from a motivated and qualified prospect who has experience in your industry. What need is there of anything more other than completing the Purchase Agreement? Well, in fact, sometimes it does happen that the buyer skips due diligence and proceeds to finalize the purchase agreement and close fairly quickly. Especially in smaller businesses that can occur more frequently. But don't count on it. It's better to be prepared for due diligence as a seller. And most buyer's attorneys should and will recommend that certain aspects of the business be checked into before the buyer commits a substantial amount of money to invest in what is for them, a new venture.

Due diligence is all about learning enough details about the business to assure a buyer that it is as clean and attractive as the Prospectus makes it seem. We all know that nothing is perfect, so this process helps the buyer understand the weaknesses as well as the strengths. It helps them confirm, or at least estimate what kind of return they can achieve. It aids in the negotiation of the details of the Purchase Agreement. It also helps them learn something about the organization and team they will obtain. It gives them a chance to find out where the "bones are buried".

A former associate of mine, a M&A attorney (Mergers & Acquisitions), once told me that every deal has negatives, or "clunkers". Due diligence is partly about finding the clunkers. I've since learned that every deal also contains surprises that the buyer didn't anticipate nor find out ahead of time, no matter how complete due diligence has been. So due diligence may not be the complete answer to finding the clunkers nor to learning of welcome opportunities. There will always ultimately be risk in every deal. But its purpose is to help the buyer minimize the risk and move forward with confidence with the purchase.

From the seller's viewpoint, due diligence can be an irritant and a distraction. But keep in mind that this process can have a major impact on the sale price of the business! Anything negative uncovered during due diligence undermines the value perception you've worked hard to create. It's important to keep in mind that if you can stay cooperative, helpful and positive throughout, this process can actually help to enhance the assurance of the value of the business. That is especially true if you have worked to prepare the business for this day, so that there are ideally no surprises and no clunkers. That is one of the reasons that business experts always recommend starting early to prepare the business AHEAD OF TIME for the day of sale.

The larger the business, the more complex due diligence may be. The process can be time consuming and costly for both parties. So for smaller businesses, due diligence is often shortened or restrained, only because the cost of the work may not be reasonable compared to the targeted purchase price. For example, an inventory count may be abbreviated to focus only on the highest value portion of the total asset. The work for the seller is in compiling records per the buyer's request, making sure they are accurate and thorough, while at the same time continuing to focus on running the business. But every business is different, and the list of items to check out will vary for every deal. The best way to illustrate the kind of potential things that can be involved, is to share a typical due diligence outline. Take a deep breath. It's a long list! But don't panic. Seldom are all these details examined. Nonetheless, the list itself provides an indication of the purpose of due diligence and the kind of information that a buyer might want to know before committing to the purchase.

DUE DILIGENCE CHECKLIST
Partially excerpted from www.accountingtools.com/due-diligence-checklist

Target Company Overview

- *Why selling?* Is the owner selling for "good" reasons, such as raising funds for an estate tax payment, a divorce, or retirement? Or for problem reasons, such as the expectation of a lawsuit, or a downward trend in the company's prospects.
- *Business plans.* Does the owner see a bright future for their own business, and does the plan have a reasonable chance of implementation?
- *Complexity.* How complex is the business? Complex businesses are difficult to grow.
- *Market review.* Review the primary players in the marketplaces in which the target competes. Also, monitor trends in the industry and the expected impact of any new technology.
- *Related acquisitions.* Have there been other acquisitions in the industry lately? What is driving these trends?
- *Reporting relationships chart.* Obtain a chart that states the reporting relationships within the business

to understand which managers are in charge of which sections.

Employees

- *Types of employees*. Obtain an organization chart.
- *Key employees*. Compile a listing of which employees actually operate the business.
- *Customer linkages*. Do any employees have such close contacts with customers that they could take the customers with them if they were to leave the company and go into business elsewhere?
- *Total compensation*. Compile the total cost of the top employees, including base pay, commissions, bonuses, stock options, payroll taxes, benefits and reimbursements.
- *Pay history*. Construct a chart detailing last pay increases, and the amount of the increase.
- *Pay freezes*. If the target company has been in financial difficulty recently, has there been pay freezes with the promise of future increases?
- *Employment agreements*. There may be agreements with some employees, under which they are entitled to severance pay if the company elects to terminate their employment.
- *Unions*. If some employees are represented by unions, obtain a copy of the union contract and peruse it for scheduled wage rate changes, work rule limitations, guaranteed benefits, and other issues that may alter the costs of the business.
- *Injury records*. If the company is involved in manufacturing or distribution, review its employee injury records.
- *Employee manual*. Always obtain a copy of the employee manual.

Employee Benefits

- *Benefits.* What medical insurance is offered to employees, and what portion of it must be paid by the employees? Is any insurance also offered to retirees? How do these benefits compare to what is offered to employees elsewhere in the acquirer's businesses?
- *Pension plan funding.* If there is a defined benefit pension plan, ascertain whether the plan is underfunded, and if so, by how much.
- *Vacations.* Determine the amount of vacation time to which each employee is entitled, and how that compares to the industry average and the company's stated vacation policy.

Financial Results

- *Annual financial statements.* Ideally, there should be financial statements for the past five years, which the team should translate into a trend-line comparison for the full five years.
- *Cash flow analysis.* A key part of the financial statements is the statement of cash flow.
- *One-time events.* If there were any operational events that are unlikely to occur again, strip them out of the results of operations. An example is one-time sales to large customers.
- *Disclosures.* Audited financial statements should include a set of disclosures on various topics. The team should review these disclosures in detail, since they can reveal a great deal more information about a company than is shown in its income statement and balance sheet.
- *Management letters.* After an audit has been completed, the auditors sometimes compile a set of recommendations into a management letter, which

they distribute to the CEO and audit committee. Any such letters issued for the past few years are worth reading.

Revenue

- *Recurring revenue stream.* A key value driver in a business is its recurring revenue stream. Determine the amount of baseline revenue that can be expected to arise on an ongoing basis.
- *Customer changes.* In the past three years, see if there is a net decline or increase in the top 10 customers, which is an indicator of the general trend of sales.
- *Available regions/channels.* Are there any likely geographic regions or distribution channels that the company has not yet entered?
- *Pricing philosophy.* How does the company set prices? Does it add a percentage profit to its costs, or set its prices based on those of competing products? Does it position its prices low, to follow a value strategy, or high, to follow a premium strategy?
- *Estimating.* Does the company have an estimating department that derives prices for customized services or products? If so, examine whether the company has persistently lost money on incorrect estimates in the past.
- *Contract terminations.* If revenues are derived from customer contracts, then obtain copies of the larger contracts and determine the remaining stream of payments related to them, when they expire, and the likelihood of obtaining follow-on contracts.
- *Accounts receivable.* Review the most recent accounts receivable aging report to see if there are

any customer invoices that are overdue by unusually long periods of time, and find out the reasons why.

Cost Structure

- *Expense trends*. Examine trends for expenses, as a percentage of sales, for example.
- *Loans to employees*. Determine the amount and nature of any loans extended to employees.
- *Fixed assets*. If there have been few fixed asset replacements in recent years, it may undermine the future competitiveness of the business. If so, then the acquirer may reduce the valuation of the company by the amount of extra investment it will have to make to bring the fixed asset base back up to a reasonable operating level.

Intellectual Property

- *Patents*. Does the company have any valuable patents?
- *Trademarks*. Has the company registered its trademarks? If not, see if someone else is using them, and whether they have trademarks or have applied for them.
- *Licensing*. Determine the size and amount of any licensing income or expense. Examine any licensing agreements.

Fixed Assets and Facilities

- *Valuation*. If the acquirer intends to sell any fixed assets, obtain a rough estimate of their actual value on the open market.
- *Utilization*. Conduct a review of the more expensive fixed assets to determine the extent of their ongoing usefulness.

- *Maintenance.* Have an experienced maintenance person examine the machinery in the production area.

Liabilities

- *Accounts payable.* Review the most recent aged accounts payable report.
- *Leases.* Determine if any equipment leases have bargain purchase clauses that allow the company to buy assets at the end of the lease period for below-market prices (such as $1).
- *Debt.* Review the debt agreements associated with outstanding debt.
- *Debts to related parties.* Have managers, owners, or shareholders loaned money to the company? What are the terms of these agreements?
- *Unrecorded liabilities.* Use interviews with the owner(s) of the company to uncover unrecorded or contingent liabilities.
- *Collateral.* Verify which assets have been designated as collateral by lenders.

Equity

- *Shareholder list.* Obtain a list of all shareholders of the company, along with the share holdings of each one.
- *Classes of stock.* Verify the stock ownership of all classes of stock, as well as the voting rights.
- *Conversion rights.* Examine all debt agreements to see if the debt holders have the right to convert the debt to shares in the company.
- *Options and warrants.* Determine the amount and terms of any stock options and warrants outstanding.

Taxes

- *Is the company continuing to pay taxes?* Review its taxes payable records to verify that payments are continuing to be made.
- *Is the company paying the correct amount of taxes?* Just because a company is remitting tax payments does not mean that those payments are correct.

Selling Activities

- *Organization.* How is the sales department organized, and how does it make sales?
- *Productivity.* Match sales records to sales personnel or storefronts to determine which sales people and/or stores are the most and least profitable.
- *Compensation plan.* How is the sales staff compensated? What is the mix of salaried versus commission pay? Does the reward system properly motivate the sales staff?
- *Skills match.* Review the types of sales occurring, and the skill level of the sales people assigned to them.

Marketing Activities

- *Comparative analysis.* How do the marketing efforts of the company compare to those of its competitors?
- *Coordination.* Is marketing coordinated with the release of new products and with the sales staff, or does it rely on general advertising?
- *Branding.* Is there a focus on branding every facet of a product's outer case, packaging, delivery, advertising, and so forth?

Materials Management

- *Supply chain.* Do the company's inventory levels match supply chain requirements?
- *Supply restrictions.* Have sales been impacted during the past five years by restrictions in the amount of certain materials? What was the impact on sales?
- *Transportation costs.* What proportion of cost of goods sold is transportation cost?
- *Supplier terminations.* Have any suppliers refused to continue doing business with the company recently. Contact them to learn why.
- *Supplier contracts.* Obtain copies of any supplier contracts or master purchase agreements in which the company commits to certain purchasing volumes over a period of time.
- *Inventory systems.* How well does the company identify, store, and keep track of its inventory?
- *Inventory obsolescence.* Be sure to examine the inventory for obsolete items, and estimate the price at which they could be disposed of.

Information Technology

- *Systems in place.* Create a complete list of all major software packages being used by the company, their versions, maintenance costs, number of users, and interfaces to other systems.
- *Licenses.* Determine the number of valid software licenses that the company has paid for.
- *Outsourcing agreements.* Review the agreements of any outsourced IT operations, to ascertain such issues as baseline services, pricing for additional services, and change of control clauses.

- *Capacity.* Investigate the usage level of existing systems, as well as the age of the equipment.
- *Customization.* What is the extent to which the company has modified any packaged software?
- *Legacy systems.* If there are custom-made software that require considerable resources to maintain, locate these systems, determine their maintenance cost, and decide whether to maintain or replace.
- *Disaster recovery plan.* Is there a disaster recovery plan that states how information is to be backed up and recovered in the event of a system failure?

Legal Issues

- *Current lawsuits.* If there are any lawsuits outstanding against the target, ascertain their status.
- *Prior lawsuits.* If there were any lawsuits within the past five years that were settled, obtain copies of the settlement agreements.
- *Legal invoices.* Review all invoices paid to law firms in the past three years.
- *Contracts review.* Examine all contracts that the target has entered into within the past five years, in particular those requiring fixed payments, royalty or commission payments.
- *Charter and bylaws.* Obtain the most recent version of the company's charter and bylaws, and review them in detail. They state voting procedures for key events, such as the sale of the business.
- *Board minutes.* Review all board minutes for the past five years.
- *Shareholder meeting minutes.* Review meeting minutes of shareholder meetings.

Purchase Agreement

Whew! You've made it through the due diligence process, and eagerly anticipate the pending sale of your business. Congratulations! You are close to the end, but now is the time to finish strong!

By this time both parties will have a pretty good idea of the details of the transaction. Assuming the attorneys of both parties have participated in the Letter of Intent and been updated or involved in due diligence, they should have a good framework for creating the Purchase Agreement. Either party's attorney can draft this agreement, but it is more often done by the buyer's attorney. Regardless of who is drafting the agreement, however, you as seller need to carefully read and understand all the terms, using your attorney to aid in that understanding. Even after a thorough due diligence examination, no one in this transaction knows your business as well as you, so you need to accept the responsibility to make sure even your own attorney understands the deal from your viewpoint and can help you get it right. That means that you need to personally review the draft Purchase Agreement, including all modifications along the way to getting a final document.

Our intent is to help you understand the process of selling your business, so all the potential aspects of a final deal as defined in your Purchase Agreement are beyond the scope of this book. However, some of the things that are commonly included in a Purchase Agreement may give you some things to think about as you contemplate preparing your business for sale.

Form of payment

Receipt of 100% of the purchase price in cash is ideal, but seldom does it work this way. For one thing, the bank financing the deal may feel more secure if the seller has a stake in the future of the business, and seek some type of seller financing of a portion of the purchase price. Seller financing is common, so some thought should be given ahead of time to what you, the seller, are comfortable with. Clearly you would prefer all the money up front in most cases, but if seller financing is required to complete the sale, ask yourself if you are willing to finance perhaps 10-30% of the price over a period of time. In many cases, even 100% seller financing is done, typically in a "land contract" type of deal.

The tax consequences of the deal also need to be considered, and here is another place where your accountant or financial adviser are vital to your team. What taxes can you expect to pay on the receipt of a substantial amount of the purchase price if it is paid to you this year? What is the overall impact of taxes if certain sums are paid in future years? There is a risk/reward tradeoff here as future payments may depend on the long-term success of the business.

What is included (or not) in the sale?
On the surface, this seems like a silly question. Everything is included in the sale, right? Well maybe not. For example, your work van also doubles as your personal camping vehicle, so you may want to hold onto it to avoid purchasing another one. But more important than some potential personal use items, there may be a reason to keep some other assets as well, most of all Accounts Receivable.

Go back to Chapter 4 on "Valuation – Sellability" and re-read the section on "Valuation Teeter-Totter". If the buyer is less sure of the collectability of accounts than the seller, the seller may want to retain these and collect the proceeds themselves. Doing so may lower the purchase price, but the tradeoff might be worthwhile. So the Purchase Agreement may contain wording that defines the cutoff date of receivables accruing to the seller.

The name of the business is another asset that the seller normally retains, especially if they've retained receivables that exist at time of closing. Understand here the difference between the legal name of the business and its trade name. The legal name is retained by the seller, but the trade name is typically sold to the buyer. For example, the assets of <u>XYZ Plastics, Inc.</u> may be sold to <u>XYZ Plastic, LLC</u>, including the trade name "<u>XYZ Plastics</u>". Note the subtle difference not only in the legal name differences, but also the letter 's' in the trade name being retained, even though the Seller has chosen a legal name for their business that doesn't use the 's'. These types of naming conventions are normal, and actually good ways to have different legal entities result from a business sale.

Of course, the trade name of the business may not be transferred in some cases, for example where the company or its product line will be absorbed into another firm with a completely different trade or corporate identity.

Another item of note about included assets concerns property ownership. A wise financial practice is that the property in which business is conducted, be owned by a separate legal entity of the owner(s). Sometimes in a business sale, the property is also sold in a separate but related transaction. But often, the seller/owner retains the property and the business continues to pay rent to the seller/owner after sale. If this is contemplated, the seller's business should already be in the practice of paying that rent so that it is seen as a normal business expense of the business being sold. That way, the buyer sees no difference between the financial return produced by the business before or after sale due to rent. The purchase agreement, then, will typically include mention of a separate lease agreement to be executed by the parties at time of closing.

Transition assistance
Often, sellers are willing to lend their assistance and expertise to a buyer for a period of time after sale. In spite of a brilliant Prospectus and thorough due diligence, there may still be aspects of the business that would benefit from the seller's knowledge. It might be related to pending or in-process projects, customer transitions, product development, personnel or a myriad of other issues. Sometimes, the assurance of seller availability as a consultant gives the buyer peace of mind that they'll be able to find help should something unforeseen arise. The purchase agreement will often define the nature of the transition assistance and how it will be compensated (retainer, salary, hourly, etc.)

Agreement not to compete
Terri sold her interior decorating business after 23 years of financial success from building a solid reputation and broad customer base. Desiring to kick back and relax with an early retirement, Terri sold her business to a young couple who eagerly looked forward to taking the business to even greater success. But after 10 months of "the good life," Terri longed for the activity and customer contact she loved and decided to start a rival decorating business competing with her old firm in the same city.

Yikes! That would be a nightmare scenario to the young couple who purchased Terri's business less than a year earlier. Clearly, buyers will want to avoid that possibility by including a non-compete clause (or separate agreement) in their purchase agreement. These usually include terms regarding the definition of what activity constitutes competition, the time frame of the agreement (perhaps 2 to 5 years) and the geographic region where the non-compete is in effect.

Representations & Warranties

Reps & warranties may look like boring, legalistic aspects of the purchase agreement, but please don't make the mistake of glossing over these and not considering their potential impact. The representations are statements that clarify the understanding that the buyer has in what the seller has represented. Should these understandings later be proven to be untrue, they could result in financial give-backs of the purchase price or in the worst case unravel the transaction all together. These statements can include anything from knowledge of health or safety hazards in the business to condition of assets. Two typical items are:

- *Environmental condition and records* – Environmental violations can lead to substantial penalties, so much so that they have the potential to shut down a business. Thus, representation is often included in purchase agreements that there are no known environmental conditions that need correcting, that no processes of the business pollute air, water or ground and that required reporting is current and complete according to legal requirements.

- *Pending or contingent lawsuits* – It might be embarrassing to admit that a disgruntled customer or former employee has threatened lawsuit but taken no action yet, but a buyer does not want a surprise of this nature to disrupt an otherwise successful venture after they take the reins. They will commonly include a representation that the seller has no knowledge of such a pending action.

Allocation of purchase price

The purchase agreement will usually reference an appended document that defines the allocation of the purchase price. The buyer and seller are agreeing that the value of the transaction will be assigned a certain way, and this is done for tax and accounting purposes and for stock valuation. What can often make allocations tricky is that what may be a good allocation for the seller, may be a poor allocation for the buyer, or vice versa. For example, if the transaction includes goodwill, sellers may want to maximize the value of it because it may be taxed at lower capital gain rates. But buyers may want to minimize the goodwill because they have to amortize it over 15 years versus the ability to depreciate other assets at a much faster rate, thus gaining near-term tax advantages.

The allocation is a fairly simple, straightforward looking document. It takes the purchase prices and divides, or allocates, value to the major elements of the sale. These may include such things as:

- Tangible property like furniture, computers, vehicles and equipment
- Value of lease
- Covenant not to compete
- Seller consulting agreement
- Goodwill
- Customer lists
- And more...

Allocation of the purchase price is typically one of the last things to occur in the selling process, but it can be one of the trickiest and most contentious areas. Often conflict is created by the advisers of the parties because the buyer and seller may have less understanding of the issues at stake and the advisers are bound and determined to win an advantage for their client. Although well meaning, all parties involved need to be willing to compromise as much as needed to complete a deal which preserves the original intent of the buyer and seller.

Chapter 7 - Teamwork

If you'd like to simplify the messages of this book into the two most important elements that lead to success in selling your business, here they are:

- <u>Start early</u>, one to five years before you hope to sell, to work on improving your business value, understanding your own motivations and laying groundwork for maximizing your selling price.
- <u>Build a team</u> of experienced advisers who can help guide you through the many nuances of a negotiation and sale.

We entrepreneurs are an independent lot, aren't we? We tend to go it alone, make our own decisions, seek our own counsel, and turn down the help and advice of others. It's in our culture, somehow. But when it comes to prepping our business for sale, finding buyers and closing the deal, nothing could be worse than trying to save a few bucks and doing this alone. Don't do it!! Allow me to remind you again, that you've spent years of your life and substantial parts of your wealth to build your successful business. It would be a shame to trip up this final chapter of your business life and "under harvest" the equity you've accumulated.

Part of your selling preparation process needs to include surrounding yourself with a few trusted advisers who are experienced in these types of transactions. The right professionals will maintain the confidentiality of your intentions and financial situation, maximize your business value and work together to avoid conflict and guide you efficiently through the process. Although the exact makeup of your team may vary based on the type of business, your own experience, availability of buyers and size of the transaction, the typical experts you should consider for your team are the following:

- *Business Coach* – Coaching for small business owners is becoming more prevalent. These experts often lead the entire selling process with you because they usually are one of the first advisers involved and because they have a wholistic awareness of your entire operation. They also help you stay focused on the ongoing business while you deal with the distractions of the sales process. Coaches also help deal with the emotional issues that creep in so that your ups and downs through the process don't undermine your goals. An experienced business coach may be exactly the right adviser to help you create your Prospectus, your Strategic Plan, your initial valuation and a related business improvement plan.

- *Accountant* – Sometimes small business owners have a good handle on their financial situation, but often that is not the case. Remember that your business's ability to make money and produce a return on investment for the new owner is top most in the buyer's mind. So having a reporting structure and performance level that reflects the attractiveness of the business is critical. Your accountant should be involved in making sure your transaction processes are accurate and complete and that your financial reports are reflective of your financial status. The accountant is also important to the valuation of the business and to the tax implications of the proceeds of the sale and the related allocation of the purchase price.

- *Attorney* – It should be clear to you that a contract or agreement confirming the sale of your business is one of the most important legal documents you will have produced during your business ownership experience. Although the buyer's attorney may do some or most of the heavy lifting creating the letter of intent and purchase agreement, you cannot rely on their professional ethics to protect your interests. It's not that a buyer's attorney will intentionally harm your status, but they are obligated to zealously and exclusively represent their client. As the seller, your attorney will be invaluable in helping to negotiate elements of the deal, examine payment options, protect your legal future and if necessary, prepare sales documents. They may also help to create or sustain your post-sale business entity and assist with tax and estate planning.

- *Financial Adviser* – For many small business owners, their business is their only retirement asset, so they may or may not have a financial adviser that they have worked with regularly. But if the sale of their business is a success, knowing the right thing to do with the proceeds is important. Even early in the planning for business sale, a financial adviser can help determine retirement financial needs so that the seller has a target price in mind that will not leave them short of their financial goals. Along with other members of the team, the financial adviser can examine payout alternatives and create investment vehicles that are best suited for the seller's situation.

- *Business Broker* – As mentioned earlier, business brokers typically work with businesses of over $1.0 - $1.5 million. For many small business owners with lower valuations, that may leave them without a viable broker to help market the business and search for potential buyers. In these cases, finding the right broker may just not be possible. In that case, the better the rest of your team can collectively help with these broker functions, the more success you'll have and the quicker the process will go. But if you are fortunate to find a broker who can help with the buyer search and the organization of the deal, it may well be worthwhile to engage with them to join your team. They are the most experienced in negotiations between buyers and sellers and can help to keep that process from unraveling, thus leading to a successful outcome.

Epilogue – A Business That Supports Your Life

In the opening chapter of this book, the Preface, it was noted that in 2011 there were 27.9 million businesses with less than 10 employees, or no employees. That is 93.5% of all business entities. If we want to define small business as less than 100 employees, then we are addressing 99.4% of business entities! Imagine that nearly all of these businesses exist in support of an owner(s) and their family. For most, it is the asset that produces their income, holds a substantial portion of their wealth, and could be the only source of money to sustain their retirement.

Yet, for many small business owners, the business is treated as little more than a job. Although their dream in starting the business may have been broader and grander, the stress and detail demands of the business over the years have whittled away their vision and hidden their original goals. It's now a job, and at that, it's a job they feel trapped in unlike their counterparts who are actually employees of someone they can tell to "take this job and shove it". It's a job they may have bought with substantial investment dollars and/or the help of a bank loan which now requires they stick with the business until those debts are paid off. It's a job that requires long hours and low pay. And it may be a job that doesn't allow much of the kind of lifestyle they envisioned as an entrepreneur.

I hope that doesn't describe you, but you know lots of people who fit that description, don't you?

What separates those who build even moderately successful businesses from those described above? They all start out pretty much the same, don't they? There are lots of answers. Some just work harder. Some have more discipline. Some manage time better. Some have better skills. Some are just lucky! And some just do a better job of holding onto their goals, keeping these goals in front of them and not allowing themselves to lose track of where they are going. They always seem to manage to put at least some of their effort into working ON their business rather than just working IN their business. As a result, they are able to build a business that supports their life, rather than spend their life supporting their business.

Some also understand that building a business that supports their life might require help. These owners are open to advice, seek out professional counsel, and collaborate with a team. They hire a coach, cultivate a mentor, or create a board of advisers. They have strong, open relationships with their accountant, banker and attorney and understand that the cost of these professionals is an investment in their success. Ironically, they find that they, the owner, still get all the credit!

So before you think about selling your business, ask yourself if you've built a business that supports your life? If it doesn't do that, consider working with a professional who is experienced in helping create more valuable businesses. If it does support your life, it probably can support someone else's life, too. So you have a sellable business! And in the final act of ownership, the business you've built may now be able to support the rest of your life as well.

Acknowledgements

The idea of writing this book grew largely out of my work with small business owners and the realization of their lack of resources to learn about or get knowledgeable help with the process of marketing, appraising, negotiating and finalizing an actual sale of their business. My interest in this topic received a big boost from John Warrillow's best-selling book, *"Built To Sell"*. John's subsequent development of his *Sellability Score* assessment tool really helped to highlight ways that business owners could improve their business and increase its eventual sales value. John's work created a foundation for me to look at the even broader picture of what business owners face in the process of selling their business.

Kudos go to AdviCoach, the franchise that got me into this business, for recognizing John Warrillow's work as an important extension of the excellent coaching tools and resources AdviCoach business coaches utilize in our work. The coaching process is one of teaching and facilitating, and it provides our clients with more motivation, more understanding and more eventual gratification in reaching their goals than a typical "consulting" approach.

Heartfelt thanks to those friends and associates who gave their personal time to read, edit and critique my work. Fellow AdviCoach Ron Nielsen has been a steady ally throughout much of my coaching career and provided an appropriate mix of encouragement and advice. My own coach and friend, Bill Michael, also provided motivation and guidance. I found it true that once you tell a couple people like Ron and Bill what you are doing and what your goal is, you create an unspoken commitment to reach the finish line.

Anyone looking for motivation need look no further than Randy Meyer, who inspires simply by his presence and his life. I greatly appreciated his review and his understanding of the purpose and intention this book serves. My friend Mark Miller brought his understanding of the small business owner and his accounting perspective to the work. Mark is a friend and associate who has also been a partner of sorts in expanding networking opportunities for small business owners in Sheboygan, Wisconsin and beyond. Shawn Rice provided outstanding critique of the book from his perspective as an attorney specializing in M&A work. Shawn is a visible and active advocate for increasing understanding about business sale transactions and value.

I am especially grateful to Karin Iwata. Karin's excitement and enthusiasm about this work came at a time when my writing motivation was at a low ebb. Her vision of the importance of the book, not only for business owners, but for me personally, was the inspiration I needed to finish the writing. I will always be appreciative of Karin's wisdom, insight and candor, not only as it applied to the critique of the book, but also related to coaching and uplifting of the small business owner.

Though I have always felt adequate as a writer, graphic art is not my forte. For that important assistance with the cover design for the book, I turned to Lynn Buehler, who understood exactly what we were trying to accomplish with a cover that attracts, while still simply conveying the idea of the book. For proofing and editing I turned to another dear friend, Mary Kay Evans, whose experience in the newspaper and printing industry was invaluable in helping me turn out a quality product that actually makes proper use of the English language.

My special assistant in my business is Sara Baltus (who also happens to be my daughter-in-law). I am blessed to have her help with software, editing, layout and many other details that she is so good at researching and figuring out. She makes me look good!

Lastly of course, I would be remiss not to thank my wife, Betsy, for understanding my desire to spend hours writing and editing in the achievement of this book. It's one thing to give up some personal time working on your business but something else to put even more effort into a project of this sort. Nothing is more important than her support and love.

About The Author

Jerry Baltus is founder and owner of Baltus Group, working to make small business stronger and their owners more successful. He is also a "coach's coach" training others in the building of their own independent businesses dedicating to helping other entrepreneurs. Baltus Group is an independent franchisee of AdviCoach, an international coaching franchise.

Jerry graduated from University of Wisconsin - Eau Claire in 1976, with a degree in Accounting. He joined Kohler Co. upon graduation and worked in the corporate accounting area of the company for four years. Taking advantage of an opportunity to do administrative work in the international sales area of the company's Generator Division, Jerry quickly became involved with distributors overseas, and became Regional Sales Manager for Latin America, traveling extensively throughout that region for two years. He was then promoted to Marketing Manager and worked closely with U.S. and foreign distributors, as well as internally on new product development with company engineers.

In 1993, Jerry became Vice President - Sales at Polar Ware Company, managing the three primary sales channels of the business, its sales team and independent sales representatives. In 2000, he was promoted to Executive Vice President and ran the day-to-day operations of the company, including Manufacturing, Engineering, HR, Accounting and IT. During this time, his business experience was enhanced further in the areas of labor management, continuous improvement, corporate acquisitions and joint ventures, as well as overall leadership.

Jerry and his wife, Betsy, live in Plymouth, WI near their two married children and six grandchildren. He is an active member of three local Chambers of Commerce, as well as Plymouth Lions Club, and BNI. He enjoys fishing and hunting, and is an avid bicyclist, logging over 2000 miles annually.

Made in the USA
San Bernardino, CA
11 January 2017